writing guides

Poetry ACTIVITIES

ALISON KELLY & YVONNE LINCOLN

POETRY FOR AGES 9–11

PHOTOCOPIABLE

CONTENTS

3 INTRODUCTION

SECTION ONE: USING GOOD EXAMPLES

4 ELDORADO
5 BEFORE THE HUNT
6 TEACHER'S NOTES
8 QUESTIONS ABOUT 'ELDORADO'
9 QUESTIONS ABOUT 'BEFORE THE HUNT'
10 DIARIES
11 I WANT TO WRITE A POEM

SECTION TWO: DEVELOPING WRITING

12 TEACHER'S NOTES
17 BUILDING POEMS
18 CONCRETE POETRY
19 TURN A HAIKU INTO A TANKA
20 DIGGING FOR MEANING
21 KENNINGS
22 ANGRY FEELINGS

SECTION THREE: WRITING

23 TEACHER'S NOTES
24 ELDORADOSCAPE
26 PHOTOGRAPH OF A CHILD
28 BUTTERFLIES

SECTION FOUR: REVIEW

30 TEACHER'S NOTES
31 IMPROVING OUR POEMS
32 MY POETIC KNOW-HOW

INTRODUCTION

The Scholastic *Writing Guides* series provides teachers with ideas and projects that promote a range of writing, bringing insights from educational research into the classroom. Each guide explores a different type of writing and provides example material, background information, photocopiable activities and teaching suggestions. Their aim is to enable teachers to guide the writing process, share planning ideas and develop themes as a context for writing activities.

The materials:
- motivate children with interesting activities
- break complex types of writing into manageable teaching units
- focus on and develop the typical features of particular types of writing
- provide original approaches to teaching.

Each book is divided into sections, beginning with examples of the type of writing being taught. These are followed by ideas for developing writing and projects that will extend over a series of sessions.

SECTION ONE: USING GOOD EXAMPLES

Section One looks at good examples of the genre, with the emphasis on using texts to stimulate and develop writing. Two example texts are shared, and questions that focus the discussion on their significant features are suggested. This is followed by activities that explore what the texts can teach us about writing, enabling teachers to compare the two texts and to go on to model the type of writing presented in the guide.

SECTION TWO: DEVELOPING WRITING

Section Two moves from reading to writing. This section provides activities that prompt and support children in planning and writing. A range of approaches includes planning templates and strategies to stimulate ideas. The activities refine children's ideas about the type of writing being developed and give them focused writing practice in the context of scaffolded tasks. Teacher's notes support each activity by explaining the objective and giving guidance on delivery.

SECTION THREE: WRITING

Section Three moves on to writing projects. Building upon the earlier work in Section Two, these projects aim to develop the quality of writing and provide a selection of ideas for class or group work on a particular theme or idea. The teacher may choose to use some or all of the ideas presented in each project as a way of weaving the strategies developed in Section Two into a more complex and extended writing task.

SECTION FOUR: REVIEW

Section Four supports the assessment process. Children are encouraged to reflect on the type of writing they are tackling and to evaluate how effectively their work has met the criteria for the genre identified in Section One.

Eldorado

Gaily bedight,
A gallant knight,
In sunshine and in shadow,
Had journeyed long,
Singing a song,
In search of Eldorado.

But he grew old –
This knight so bold –
And o'er his heart a shadow
Fell as he found
No spot of ground
That looked like Eldorado.

And, as his strength
Failed him at length,
He met a pilgrim shadow:
"Shadow," said he,
"Where can it be,
This land of Eldorado?"

"Over the mountains
Of the Moon,
Down the valley of the
Shadow,
Ride, boldly ride,"
The shade replied,
"If you seek for Eldorado."

Edgar Allan Poe

Before the Hunt

Howling wind,
    hear me,
Dancing trees,
    hail me,
Cooling breeze,
    calm me,
Guiding sky
    light my
way through the bush.
    As the stars
protect the lonely moon
    So may I
escape the snares
    in this living forest
    As the cat
stalks its prey
So may I
Be first to spy my game
    Living forest hear me
Chilling wind still my heart
Teasing shadows smile with me
Lead me to my hunt.

Lari Williams (Nigeria)

SECTION ONE
USING GOOD EXAMPLES

Before we embark on teaching children how to write poetry, we need to discuss with them what poetry actually is. One way to initiate this is to ask them how poetry is different from other kinds of writing, list their responses and then use this list to generate a definition – perhaps for the benefit of a younger child or, as one teacher has suggested, of a Martian! There are many famous sayings about poetry, and you might find some of these useful to share and discuss with the class. For example:
- *'The best words in the best order' (Coleridge)*
- *'the spontaneous overflow of powerful feelings' (Wordsworth)*
- *'Language pared to its essentials' (WH Auden)*
- *'the song and dance in the words' (T Hughes)*

The activities in this section, and throughout this book, focus on helping children to understand and use some of the key characteristics of poetry: rhythm, structure, figurative devices, different poetic forms, the expression of emotions, and the subtle and multi-layered nature of poetic writing.

Sharing the texts

Eldorado

The American writer Edgar Allan Poe (1809–1849) is probably best known for his weird and melancholic short stories. In this poem on photocopiable page 4 he turns his skills to writing about the quest for the mythical city of Eldorado. The legend has it that *Eldorado* (meaning 'the gilded') was the name given to a South American king who was covered in oil and then sprinkled with gold dust. Over the years, the name has come to mean an elusive city of gold that has been the goal of many fruitless expeditions in search of its treasures. It is often used to symbolise futile 'get-rich-quick' enterprises.

In this tightly structured narrative poem, Poe uses the word *shadow* in each verse with subtle changes of meaning as the knight's search becomes increasingly desperate. Note that Poe's southern American accent would have shortened the 'a' in *Eldorado*, thus providing a truer rhyme with *shadow* than an English pronunciation gives. The shift in the meaning of *shadow* from verses 1 to 2 is from a literal to a metaphorical use. Then, in verse 3, the knight seems to meet the embodiment of a shadow, whose guidance in the final verse could be read as leading the knight on to his inevitable death and/or to the goal of his quest. It's for the children to bring their own interpretations to bear here. This is a poem brimming with hidden stories, and the questions on photocopiable page 8 are intended to help the children start thinking about some of these.

Give the children copies of page 4, and display an OHT or A3 copy of photocopiable page 8. Start a shared session by reading the poem aloud together at least twice, and asking the children for any words they do not recognise. Explain these – for example, *bedight* means 'adorned' or 'decked out'. Now take each verse in turn and ask the children what pictures they see; this is best done through individual reading and then sharing in pairs before moving back to whole-class discussion. Choose from the question prompts on page 8 as necessary, and use the circles to record key words from the children's feedback. Ask the children for their understanding of the way the word *shadow* is used in each verse.

Now focus on the poem's rhyme scheme and structure, asking the children what patterns they can spot. Label the rhyming lines – for example, the first verse has the pattern AABCCB. Note the different pattern in the final verse. Can the children suggest reasons for the change in rhythm? (For example, the knight's fading strength.) Ask them why the poem has a rapid, regular beat (perhaps to echo a horse's hooves).

Finally, as a shared writing activity, write an additional verse with the same rhyme scheme and repetitions of *shadow* and *Eldorado*. This verse could precede the first verse, or come between verses 1 and 2, or follow on from the final verse. In writing such a verse the children have an opportunity to infer and tell some of the hidden stories that they think this poem suggests.

Before the Hunt
In contrast to the narrative purpose of 'Eldorado', the powerful Nigerian poem on photocopiable page 5 has the purpose of an incantation or prayer. It relies on pattern and repetition, rather than a formal rhyme scheme, for its poetic effect. The poem is structured in three distinct sections. It starts with gently paced appeals from the hunter for protection from the elements. Then the rhythm changes in a section shaped around two similes. The final four lines echo the first section, but the pace is increased by combining the pattern of the first lines into longer lines. Here the language conveys a sense of the danger that lies ahead as the hunter prepares to confront the *chilling wind* and the *teasing shadows*.

Give the children copies of the poem on photocopiable page 5. Start by reading the poem aloud in sections, using an OHT or A3 copy of it to show the divisions: half of the class read lines 1–9, the other half read lines 10–18, and everyone reads the final four lines. Discuss the repetition and the use of imperatives; how do these affect the way the poem should be read? Compare lines 8 and 9 with lines 2, 4 and 6 to help the children appreciate the change of rhythm.

Display an OHT or A3 copy of photocopiable page 9. As with 'Eldorado', use the questions on this sheet to prompt the children's own responses to the poem. Record these on the sheet, encouraging the class to tease out what lies behind the poem. Spend some time identifying the different kinds of figurative language in the poem: metaphor (*lonely moon*), simile (*As the cat...*) and personification (*shadows smile*).

As a shared writing activity, reorganise the last four lines to follow the pattern of the first nine. How does this change the way it would be read aloud?

Taking ideas further

Diaries
The activity on photocopiable page 10 builds on the children's responses to the two poems. Here the purpose is to develop their appreciation of the different impacts, effects and meanings of the two poems by making them compare these elements. As they write the knight's diary entry, the children will use an anticipatory tone echoing that of 'Before the Hunt'. This will contrast with the hunter's diary entry reflecting on his adventures. The children are asked to write in prose at this point, as the focus is on their ideas. This activity is meant to fine-tune the children's understanding of poetry in anticipation of the writing to come. Finally, use the children's writing to discuss the differences between their prose and the poems. Try to draw out some general points about the differences between poetry and prose.

I want to write a poem
Photocopiable page 11 shows a series of questions with possible answers, representing the decisions that the children will need to make when writing a poem. It guides them through the process of choosing a topic, deciding on an appropriate form and thinking about the stylistic devices they might use. All of the features listed here are covered in more detail in Section Two. Enlarge the poster to A3 size. You could display it in the middle of an empty board, so that the children can surround it with examples of the different poetic features as they find them (written on Post-It Notes).

ONE: USING GOOD EXAMPLES

Questions about 'Eldorado'

VERSE 1

What does the knight look like?
What is he wearing?
What is he carrying?
What colours do you think of?
What is the expression on his face?
Why is he on this journey?
What are his hopes and fears?
What does 'shadow' mean in this verse?

VERSE 2

What does the knight look like now?
How is he feeling?
What is he carrying?
What is the expression on his face?
What has happened to him on his journey?
What does 'shadow' mean in this verse?

VERSES 3 AND 4

Who do you think the pilgrim shadow is?
Do you think that the knight is near Eldorado?
Will he ever get there?
What does the pilgrim shadow know?
How do you think the knight is feeling now?

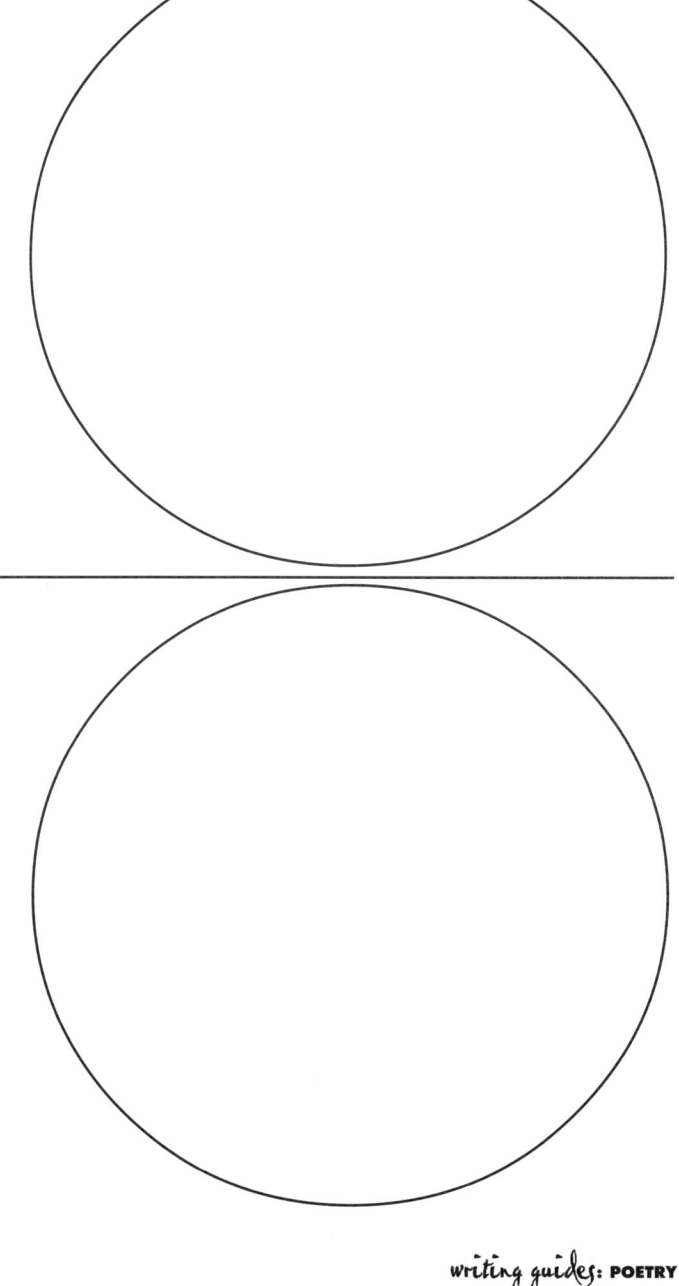

8   SCHOLASTIC PHOTOCOPIABLE   writing guides: POETRY

Questions about 'Before the Hunt'

Who is speaking in the poem?

What do you think the hunter is feeling?

What is being hunted?	Where is the hunt?	Why is it happening?

Why is the hunter saying this poem?

Diaries

1. Write a diary entry for the knight in 'Eldorado'.

You are about to set out on the quest for Eldorado. Your horse is ready and your bags are packed. This is the last diary entry you will make from your home. What are your hopes and fears? Who will you miss? What adventures do you think you will have? Do you think it will be easy to reach Eldorado?

2. Write a diary entry for the hunter in 'Before the Hunt'.

You have returned from the hunt. You are very tired, but want to write about it all. Was the hunt successful? How did you feel when you were alone and seeking prey? How are you feeling now? What was the best moment of the hunt? What was the most frightening moment?

I want to write a poem

What will I write about?

my family   my friends

my school   my feelings   a story   things I have done

things I hate   things I really like   things I have seen

What form will my poem take?

Will it rhyme?   Will I use repetition?

I could write a…

kenning   story poem   tanka

rhyming poem   concrete poem   haiku

What kinds of language will I use?

personification

metaphor   assonance   onomatopoeia   alliteration

Now I will write…

SECTION TWO
DEVELOPING WRITING

The first section of this book introduced the children to some of the key features of poetry: different poetic forms and figurative devices; the use of pattern, rhyme and rhythm; and the use of poetry to express feelings. This section allows the children to explore and rehearse these features.

As a backdrop to the activities in this section, it is essential that you establish a strong classroom ethos in which poetry has high status and is seen as an important part of children's literacy work. Opportunities to read poems aloud to the class should be seized as often as possible – reading aloud provides a significant route for children to tune into the language, rhythms and voices of poetry. Set up a poets' corner or poetry area with a focus on a particular poet, anthology, poetic form or poem. Include the poster from photocopiable page 11, poetry recordings and a notice board alerting children to new contributions (such as the children's own poems). You could set up another board on which children stick Post-It Notes with their requests for a poem to be read aloud (specifying who should read it). Share your own favourite poems. Make class anthologies of the children's favourite poems for the book corner or for a younger class.

The children should develop poetry portfolios in which to keep their drafts, exercises, jottings and ideas. They could start these by listing some terms from the poster in readiness for making glossaries over the next few weeks. As homework, they could write out a favourite poem for their front cover.

One danger of teaching children to write poetry is that a focus on form and language can distract them from one of the main purposes of poetry: to convey strong and diverse emotions. An over-emphasis on technical aspects reduces the process to a mechanistic and skills-based one. The last two activities in this section help children to appreciate the affective dimension of poetry.

THE BEST WORDS

OBJECTIVE
■ To focus on identifying and using figurative devices.

WHAT YOU NEED
Photocopiable pages 4 and 5 (one poem per pair), board or flip chart, paper, writing materials.

WHAT TO DO
You may wish to recap on the earlier discussion of figurative language (see page 7) to make sure that the children have a secure understanding of the terms *alliteration*, *metaphor*, *simile* and *personification*. The emphasis in this activity is on collaborative discussion. The children work in groups of four; one pair looks at 'Eldorado' and the other at 'Before the Hunt'. Ask them to look for examples of alliteration, metaphor, simile and personification. Why do they think the poet used these devices? The group discuss what they have found. Now write the following on the board:

'Eldorado'		'Before the Hunt'
knight	SIMILE	trees
shadow	ALLITERATION	sky
moon	PERSONIFICATION	stars
horse	METAPHOR	
shadows		

Ask the pairs to imagine they are the author of the poem they were reading before. Can they use these devices in new ways to describe the things listed? Their ideas can be shared with the class, and compared with the language of the poems.

SNAP!
WHAT YOU NEED
An A4 sheet of card cut up into 12 cards for each pair of children, scissors, writing materials.

WHAT TO DO
In this activity, the children practise the skills used in 'The best words' in the context of making and trialling a 'Snap' game for a younger class (perhaps Year 4).

Give each pair of children a set of 12 cards. Work with the children to write examples of simile, metaphor and personification on the first three cards. For example, using the theme of food: *a mountain of sandwiches* (metaphor); *She ate like a horse* (simile); *Sausages burst angrily in the frying pan* (personification). Now ask the children to think of their own examples on the same theme to fill the remaining blank cards. You may need to recap on the definitions of these terms. For children with less experience, you could provide more examples (such as *popcorn popping like gunshots*). The children should then play the game (by calling out *Snap!* when they see two similes, two metaphors and so on) before trying it out with younger children.

As an extension, the children could also make 'Snap' games for other types of figurative language such as onomatopoeia, alliteration and assonance.

OBJECTIVE
- To gain a secure understanding of simile, metaphor and personification.

MY FAVOURITE MEAL
WHAT YOU NEED
Writing materials, paper, a list of possible prompts such as *waterfalls of milk* and *cascades of sugar*, a writing frame if necessary (see below).

WHAT TO DO
Working in pairs, the children should select their favourite meal and list some of its ingredients. They then work on a figurative description of each ingredient. Suggest that they write each description on a new line, creating a poem.

For children who need more support, you might like to provide a writing frame to structure their thinking. For example:

Breakfast cereal
As crunchy as ………
…………….. of milk
Sugar like ……………

OBJECTIVE
- To use figurative language in a descriptive poem.

BUILDING POEMS (1)
WHAT YOU NEED
Photocopiable page 17 (one copy per child), writing materials, including coloured pens or crayons.

WHAT TO DO
If you are working with a guided group, ask them to read out the verse from Kit Wright's poem on photocopiable page 17 together, then ask them what they notice about the rhythm and rhyme. Make sure they are clear about how to divide up the verse. However, the children could work on this sheet independently. The bottom line of the sheet provides some optional suggestions to support less confident children, and can be cut off if you feel these are not necessary.

OBJECTIVE
- To appreciate how the structure of a poem can contribute to its meaning.

OBJECTIVE

■ To understand the role that repetition can play in structuring and patterning poems.

BUILDING POEMS (2)
WHAT YOU NEED
A selection of words, phrases and sentences that could be repeated for effect – for example: words: *teachers, playtimes, chips*; pairs of words: *exciting/boring, rainy/sunny*; phrases: *a good friend, sizzling chips*; sentences: *It's really annoying. Don't do that*; incomplete sentences: *And then the teacher said… But why…?*

WHAT TO DO
Use any of the above to model in shared writing how particular words, phrases or sentences can be used as structuring devices through repetition. For example:

> Teachers
> In the classroom on Monday
> Always grumpy
> Teachers
> In the playground on Tuesday
> Always bossy
> Teachers…

The children go on to try this out for themselves, using your pattern and/or specific ideas or their own. Give them as much support as they need (for example, by suggesting a pair of contrasting words to help them structure each new verse).

OBJECTIVE

■ To develop appreciation of the structure and patterning devices that poets use.

JIGSAWS
WHAT YOU NEED
Scissors, writing materials, large pieces of sugar paper, a selection of poems cut up into sections for the children to reassemble. Vary the size of the sections and the complexity of the poems to differentiate the activity. Use poems whose pattern and structure are very evident (for example, they have a regular rhyme scheme, tell a clearly-defined story; use repetition and/or consist of equal-length verses). You could model this using 'Eldorado' or 'Before the Hunt'. Other suitable poems include many in Robert Louis Stevenson's collection *A Child's Garden of Verses*.

WHAT TO DO
The purpose of this activity is to help the children see how patterning, repetition and structure are cohesive devices: they hold a poem together. The children should work in groups of two to four, with a single cut-up poem per group. When they have decided on the best layout, they should stick the strips onto a sheet of sugar paper and label the clues that they used (rhymes, line breaks, repeated lines and so on). The reconstructed poems can be shared in a plenary session. Emphasise that the children's reasons for choosing their layout are what matters, not whether it exactly matches the original.

In a follow-up session, the children could choose examples of structured poems, cut them up and give them to other children to reconstruct. Discuss what clues the children provided and followed.

In another follow-up activity, pairs of children could work on the computer with a poem that you have typed in without division into lines. They can use the ENTER key to decide where the breaks should go, inserting extra breaks for the gaps between verses. They can print out their work without saving the document, so that it reverts back for the next pair.

CONCRETE POETRY

WHAT YOU NEED
Photocopiable page 18, examples of concrete poetry – for example, from *The Works* edited by Paul Cookson (Macmillan) or Edwin Morgan's *Selected Poems* (Carcanet), writing materials.

WHAT TO DO
Share some examples of concrete poetry with the class before the children embark on this activity in groups or pairs. You may need to distinguish between a concrete poem (where the shape of the poem reflects its theme) and calligrams (where the print itself reflects the theme, as in bigger). You need to emphasise that drawing the shape of the poem is just a planning tool: the real skill lies in shaping the poem appropriately.

Hand out copies of photocopiable page 18, telling the children to follow the instructions on the sheet. You could display the finished concrete poems or remind the children to put them in their poetry portfolios.

OBJECTIVE
■ To learn about concrete poetry and develop understanding of form.

TURN A HAIKU INTO A TANKA

WHAT YOU NEED
Photocopiable page 19, examples of haiku (for example, from *The Works*), writing materials.

WHAT TO DO
Remind the children what the features of haiku are: three lines organised with a pattern of five, seven and five syllables. Some them some examples of haiku. Photocopiable page 19 explains how the tanka form developed from the haiku. The children have to add their own additional two lines to the familiar scenario presented in the haiku. They then go on to write their own haiku for a friend to turn into a tanka. You might like to tell the children that a feature of the traditional Japanese haiku is that one of the words in the poem is seasonal. Note that where haiku have been translated from Japanese, the syllable count may differ from the strict pattern.

OBJECTIVE
■ To understand what haiku and tanka are.

DIGGING FOR MEANING

WHAT YOU NEED
Photocopiable page 20, writing materials.

WHAT TO DO
In the poem by Ezra Pound shown on photocopiable page 20, the image of a discarded fan evokes the possibility that its owner is also rejected. The imagery is cold and sharp, enhancing the bleak mood of the poem. Use the questions on the sheet to guide a discussion, from which the children should record key words and phrases on the sheet. It is very important that the children develop their own ideas about the poem, rather than expecting there to be a 'right' answer. The focus here is on interpreting the poem, but questions about form may also arise. For instance, why has Pound decided not to write a perfect haiku?

OBJECTIVE
■ To understand that poetry is often written at different levels, and that a poet may deliberately conceal meaning to allow for different interpretations.

TWO: DEVELOPING IDEAS

OBJECTIVES
- To understand what kennings are.
- To describe something in the style of a kenning.

KENNINGS

WHAT YOU NEED
Photocopiable page 21, writing materials, individual whiteboards (optional).

WHAT TO DO
You may wish to use a shared writing session to introduce kennings. Model an example, such as: *Mouse... cat hater... cheese nibbler*. Write up some of the children's ideas, then ask them to write some more on their whiteboards. Then ask them to work individually on photocopiable page 21.

The children's kennings can be displayed with each kenning written on a piece of paper that makes a flap over an illustration of the kenning's theme.

OBJECTIVES
- To use the medium of poetry to express their own feelings.
- To recognise other poets' expressions of feeling.

ANGRY FEELINGS (1)

WHAT YOU NEED
Photocopiable page 22, writing materials, *The Puffin Book of Utterly Brilliant Poetry* edited by Brian Patten (optional), some poems about anger.

WHAT TO DO
A warm-up to this activity could be provided through a 'circle time' discussion about things that make us angry or upset.

Before the children start work on photocopiable page 22, explain that some poetry is written to express different kinds of feelings. The sheet asks the child to write a short poem, and you may wish to provide some additional guidance with this. For example, point out that Rosen uses short sentences and active verbs, writes in the present tense and records the actual words that people say. If possible, read the whole poem from which this extract is taken ('I'm the Youngest in Our House' in *The Puffin Book of Utterly Brilliant Poetry*), along with other poems that tackle feelings.

When the children have written their poems, they could read them aloud, and explore the feelings further by hot-seating or role-playing some of the situations.

OBJECTIVE
- To use the medium of poetry to express their own feelings.

ANGRY FEELINGS (2)

WHAT YOU NEED
Writing materials.

WHAT TO DO
In guided group work, remind the children about the angry poems they have written. Now go on to explore different emotions (such as fear, misery, joy and suspicion) with the children, talking about how we can use our senses to describe different moods. For instance, when talking about fear, ask them: *How does your skin feel when you are very frightened? What colours does fear make you think of? What sounds are frightening?*

The children can go on to write their own poems about a particular emotion. Be ready to give them prompts to structure their work if necessary. For example: *I feel miserable when... My misery feels like... My misery is the colour of... Misery is the sound of...* You could also prompt them to use figurative language: *My misery is like... My misery is a...*

writing guides: **POETRY**

Building poems

How is this verse of a poem built? Can you find the patterns?

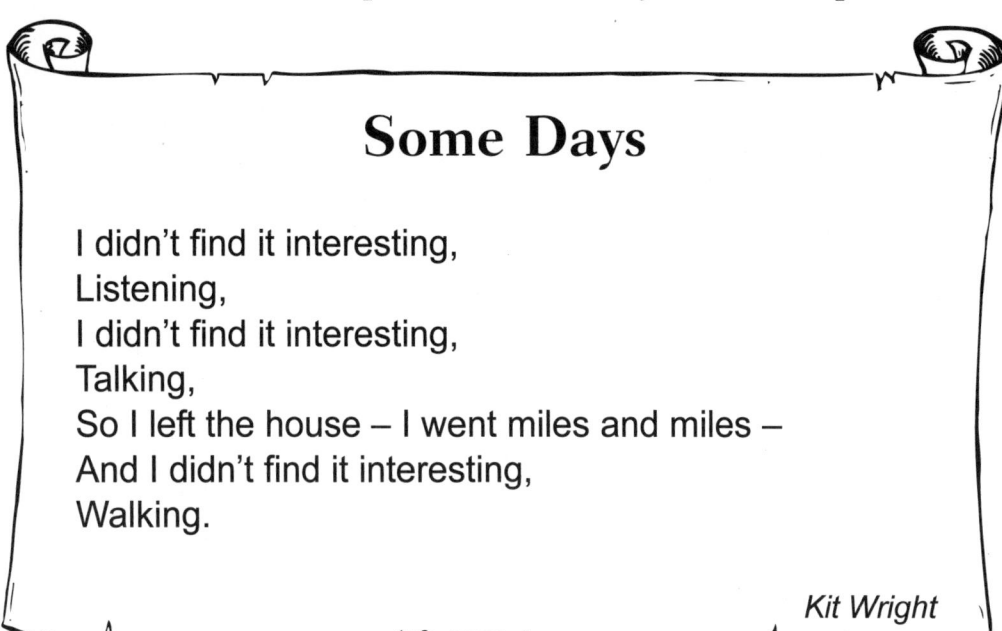

Some Days

I didn't find it interesting,
Listening,
I didn't find it interesting,
Talking,
So I left the house – I went miles and miles –
And I didn't find it interesting,
Walking.

Kit Wright

Use different-coloured pencils to colour in words or groups of words so that they show a pattern. How has Kit Wright used repeated words or sounds to build this verse of his poem?

Now try to write a similar verse.

I didn't find it…

reading fishing sleeping writing eating running bumping laughing

Concrete poetry

A concrete poem is a poem that is arranged on the page to look like the subject of the poem. For example:

```
tiny
   drops
       of
   d      rain
   r
   i        d
   z        o
   z        w
   l        n
   e
```

Now write your own concrete poem for a subject to do with the weather. Choose from:

| snow | ice | frost | wind | sun | rainbow | fog |

Planning tip
It might help you to sketch the shape of your poem first, then plan the poem using your sketch.

When you're happy with your plan, write the poem out again without the sketch.

Turn a haiku into a tanka

A tanka is a short poem. It is made up from a haiku by adding two extra lines of seven syllables each. Haiku were first written by members of the court in Japan, who would send their haiku to a friend. The friend would respond by adding two lines to make a tanka.

Turn this haiku into a tanka:

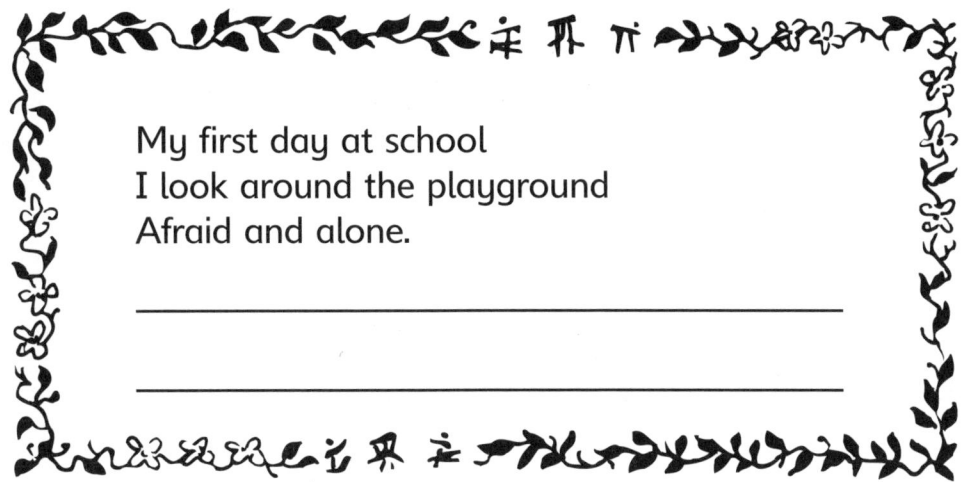

My first day at school
I look around the playground
Afraid and alone.

_____

_____

Now find or write another haiku. Give it to a friend to turn into a tanka.

Digging for meaning

> **Fan-Piece, for her Imperial Lord**
> *by Ezra Pound*
>
> O fan of white silk
> Clear as frost on the grass blade
> You also are laid aside

What do you see when you read this poem?
Where might this be taking place? What are the clues?
Is this a sad or happy poem? How can you tell?
What might have happened? Why?
What might the owner of the fan say?
Can you tell the story that led up to this poem?
What might happen next?

Kennings

Read these two kennings.

Cat

Bird watcher
Mouse pouncer
Spider teaser
Burr-tongued hisser
Duvet tester
Sun worshipper
Night prowler

Dog

Bone chewer
Slipper taker
Loyal looker
Intruder alarm
Park racer
Wind chaser
Happy panter

Kennings have been written since Viking times.
Can you write a definition of what a kenning is and what it does?

A kenning is...

Now write your own kenning.
You can choose one of these titles, or find a subject of your own.

teeth   ears   nose   thumbs   eyes   toes   elbows   eyebrows

Here is an example:

Teeth
Apple crunchers
Toffee wrestlers
Tongue guards

Angry feelings

Here are the last few lines of a poem by Michael Rosen called 'I'm the Youngest in Our House'. It is about a child who has been told to do something that the child does not want to do.

> **Now I'm angry. I am angry
> So I say – what shall I say?
> I say
> 'Shuttup, Stinks
> YOU CAN'T RULE MY LIFE.'**

What do you think this child has been told to do?

_____

Talk with a friend about things that you get told to do that make you angry.

Write some words on the lines below to describe your anger and how you feel.

_____
_____
_____
_____
_____

In the speech bubbles, write what you might say.

Use some of your ideas to write a short poem about being angry.
Try to finish your poem by using Michael Rosen's lines. Put in your own words instead of 'Shuttup, Stinks…'

Section Two sharpens the children's understanding of ways of shaping words and ideas in poetic forms. Section Three builds on this understanding as the children move on to develop more crafted poems. This section provides contexts for writing poetry: there are three separate sets of activities, each stemming from a different context. Authentic poetry writing depends on far more than the mere application of a discrete set of skills; genuine audiences and contexts are needed that will engage the children's interests and emotions.

Hooking the interest of boys is a particular concern in the teaching of poetry. The first set of activities stem from the story of the knight in 'Eldorado'; and a photograph of a boy provides the central image for the second activity. The final activity draws on an imaginative story about a girl.

SECTION THREE
WRITING

Eldoradoscape

Allow the children to revisit 'Eldorado' (from Section One) before embarking on photocopiable pages 24–5. They should re-read the poem and be reminded of the hidden meanings they uncovered in the class discussion (see page 6), as well as referring to their poetry portfolios from Section Two. The purpose of this activity is to write a series of poems that are linked thematically – in this case, by the narrative of Poe's poem. The double-page spread provides an evocative visual context for creating and displaying the poems. This activity is probably best carried out by pairs, so that each pair can share the task of completing the landscape. More confident children could tackle all the poems individually. The children could use a spare copy of the sheet, rough paper or an exercise book for drafting.

Photograph of a child

A powerful photographic image provides the context for writing the next poem. The children write a poem in order to articulate some of the emotions that the image prompts. The photograph on photocopiable page 26 was taken in 1957 and published with the title *Boy on a Bomb Site*. Note that this information is not provided for the children, as it might pre-empt their interpretations. You may decide to reveal the title and date later (perhaps as part of a display of the children's work). The image is rich in possible interpretations. The little boy might really be distressed, or he might be playing hide-and-seek. There are powerful clues about untold stories: the bandaged knee, the debris in which he is standing, the foraging boys in the background.

The children can work in pairs, with individual copies of the photo (page 26) and the instruction sheet (page 27). They should record key words and ideas from an initial discussion to form the basis of their poems. You may wish to suggest that they use particular forms. An alternative approach might be to structure the poem around two verses, each prompted by the ideas in section 4 of the sheet: one verse starts with the boy's feelings and the other with the feelings of the child reading. The children should also look at their earlier poems about feelings (see page 16).

Butterflies

Kevin Crossley-Holland's short story on photocopiable page 28 supplies the context for writing two poems. If possible, read the story with the class in an earlier shared reading session, and look at features such as colour words and movement words. Give each child a copy of the story and the instruction sheet (photocopiable page 29). Writing the first poem involves focusing on the noises that surround the girl at the beginning of the story, and creating a repetitive poem by using a line from the story as an anchoring device (see 'Building poems (2)' in Section Two). The second activity involves identifying some key features of the language used in the story, and planning and writing a short poem that uses these features.

writing guides: POETRY

THREE: WRITING

Eldoradoscape

Eldoradoscape

24 SCHOLASTIC PHOTOCOPIABLE — writing guides: POETRY

1. Re-read 'Eldorado'.

2. Write a sequence of poems to put on this 'Eldoradoscape':

- a **kenning** for the moon
- a **concrete poem** for the mountains
- a **haiku** for the knight
- a **tanka** for the shadow
- a short poem for the horse (with a regular **rhythm** for the hoofbeats).

3. Try to use some of these in your poems: **personification, metaphor, simile, alliteration, assonance.**

Photograph of a child

1. Look at the photograph. Brainstorm all the feelings and words that it makes you think of. Write them round the photograph, adding arrows if you need to.

2. Now talk with a partner about these questions:

- Who do you think this child is?
- Where do you think the photograph was taken?
- What do you think the child is feeling?
- What do you think he might say if he were to speak now?
- What would you like to say to him?
- If this were a single frame from a film, what do you think the frames before and after would show?

3. Now share your ideas with another pair. You may find that you have very different ideas about what is going on in the photograph.

4. Plan a poem about this photograph. For your opening line, use either what you think the little boy would say or what you would say.

Also include in your poem:

- something about the little boy's feelings, and maybe yours as well
- something about the ideas that you've discussed with your partner.

5. Before you start writing, read the poems that you wrote about feelings. Can you use any of the techniques that you tried out then?

Butterflies

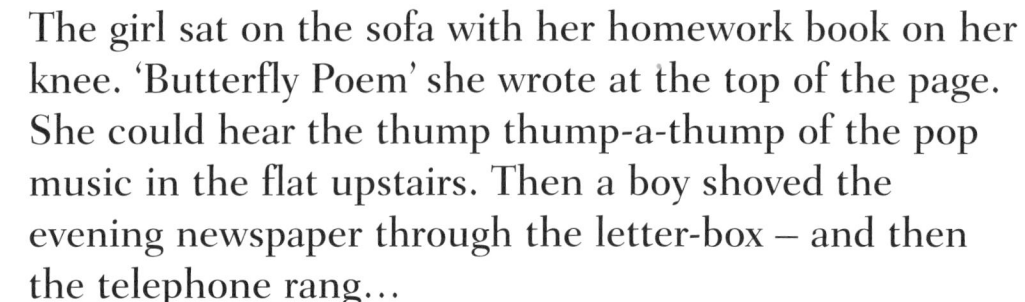

The girl sat on the sofa with her homework book on her knee. 'Butterfly Poem' she wrote at the top of the page. She could hear the thump thump-a-thump of the pop music in the flat upstairs. Then a boy shoved the evening newspaper through the letter-box – and then the telephone rang…

How difficult it was to concentrate.

But after a while the girl caught a few colourful words and set them down on her white page. Then some more. And the more words she caught, the easier they became to catch, the best words in the world.

Next morning, the girl got ready to go to school. She opened her homework book and flicked to the page headed 'Butterfly Poem'. But where were the words? They had all gone. The girl looked at her book in amazement – she turned it upside down, she checked no page had been torn out, she leafed through it in case the words had somehow escaped to another page…

Then it seemed to the girl as if her arms and legs were made of air, and her head was rising through the ceiling. She kissed her mum goodbye and closed the front door…

The girl rubbed her eyes. She screwed them up and opened them again. All around her were little scraps of orange and turquoise and jasmine and violet: the whole grey street where she lived was quick and brightly coloured with hundreds and thousands of butterflies.

Kevin Crossley-Holland

from *Short! A Book of Very Short Stories* (OUP)

Butterfly poems

Use the story 'Butterflies' as the starting point for writing two poems.

Poem 1: 'How difficult it was to concentrate…'
The story describes some of the noises that distracted the girl when she was trying to write her poem. List these below, and then add some more ideas of your own. Use **alliteration**, **assonance** and **onomatopoeia** wherever you can.

Thump thump-a-thump…

Now use the line 'How difficult it was to concentrate…' as many times as you want, to give your poem a pattern. Work this out on a new sheet of paper, then write a final version on another sheet.

Poem 2: 'The best words in the world'
Now you're going to use some words and ideas from the story in a poem.

- Start by highlighting some especially good words or phrases that you might use in your poem (for example, highlight 'colour words' in yellow).
- In a different colour, highlight some interesting words that are used to describe movement (for example, 'caught').
- Now think of at least one powerful metaphor or simile that could help you to describe a butterfly.

Now you're ready to write your poem. Write one of these three:

- a concrete poem
- a kenning about butterflies
- a poem that tells part of the story, using and repeating some of the words you've highlighted to make a rhythm.

Plan your poem on the back of this sheet, then write your final version on a new sheet of paper.

SECTION FOUR
REVIEW

This section gives children and teachers an opportunity to assess the development of the children's skills and the progress they have made in writing poetry. It invites children to evaluate, discuss and argue about what they have learnt, and to practise using various types of poems and features that make up a poem. It is only through discussion of the children's work that the teacher can see how the children's understanding of ways in which poetry can be used to express emotions is developing; these things are clearly not measurable.

This section presents pupil activities that allow for self-evaluation, rethinking and redrafting, as well as providing time to celebrate and share their skills and achievements with others. There is the option of some elements (see page 32) being used for summative assessment, should you require this.

The photocopiable review pages are checklists that form the basis of a record of the children's development in the writing of poetry. They will provide a summary of the work covered, and are intended to give the teacher a clear picture of individual development when viewed alongside the children's poetry portfolios.

Review activities

Improving our poems

Photocopiable page 31 provides the children with two tables which they can fill in as part of their own self-assessment of completed and ongoing work, after discussion with their writing partner or critical friend. The first table asks questions about the child's work. The second table provides the child and the teacher with a list of targets for redrafting. These may take the form of changing a word, redrafting a line or two, using a particular poetic device or changing the structure.

My poetic know-how

Photocopiable page 32 relates to the children's knowledge of poetic devices and forms. The first table requires them to write definitions of poetic devices (such as metaphor) that they have become familiar with. The second table could be used by the teacher to assess the individual child's understanding of poetic forms (such as concrete poems) that they have been learning about. This could be completed without any reference to the children's portfolios, giving the teacher clear knowledge of what the children have learnt regarding terminology and what still needs to be taught or clarified.

Poetry and portfolios

The final assessment of the children's work will be the actual portfolios that the children have produced by the end of this series of activities. This would include their own redrafting after discussion with others, as well as work that has been produced in a group. By looking through the work together, both the teacher and the child should be able to recognise the development of skills and the handling of words within patterns to express ideas, moods and descriptions. These portfolios should be a clear reflection of the children's achievements. They should inspire feelings of pride and satisfaction as the children recognise their own crafting of poems, their mastering of techniques and their ability to orchestrate 'the best words in the best order'.

Improving our poems

Choose a poem that you are writing, or one that you have finished.

Talk about your poem with a partner, using these questions for discussion and making short notes as you talk.

Have you made good use of the form you have chosen?	
Have you used metaphors, similes or personification?	
Have you used alliteration, assonance or onomatopoeia?	
Have you used any of these too much?	
Have you expressed the feelings that you wanted to?	
Have you chosen the best words?	
Have you put your words into the best order?	

Share your ideas, and then fill in the table below to help you with your poem.

Bits of the poem I need to work on	What I'm going to do

My poetic know-how

I can explain these types of language:

metaphor	
simile	
personification	
assonance	
alliteration	
onomatopoeia	

I can explain these types of poem:

concrete poem	
haiku	
tanka	
kenning	